Mission to Millions

10 Strategies to Budget Your Money

Curtis G Martin

10 STRATEGIES TO BUDGET YOUR MONEY

www.curtisGmartin.com

Publisher
Back House Books
Los Angeles, CA
United States

Printed in the United States of America

Send E-mail for Booking

Curtis G Martin

to

Info@curtisGmartin.com

Check out the website at

www.CURTISGMARTIN.com

DEDICATION

To Malia, Mia, and Milo,

This book isn't just a collection of strategies; it's a gift. It's a financial compass, a blueprint I created for you to navigate the world of money confidently. Remember our conversations about saving, spending wisely, and setting goals? This book captures those lessons and offers practical tools to implement them.

Life is an incredible adventure, filled with dreams you'll chase and experiences you'll crave. This book equips you with the knowledge to manage your finances effectively, ensuring financial worries don't sidetrack your dreams. Financial freedom isn't just about having money; it's about having choices. It's about knowing your hard work is building a secure future for yourself and the ability to pursue your passions without fear.

With each page you turn, I hope you discover the power of budgeting and the sense of accomplishment it brings. Remember, above all, to be smart with your money, but most importantly, have fun exploring the world of finance!

With all my love, your dad,

Curtis G Martin

Foreword

Do you ever feel like your hard-earned money slips through your fingers faster than you can track it? Are you tired of living paycheck to paycheck, with dreams on hold due to financial uncertainty?

This book, "10 Strategies to Budget Your Money," stands out. It's not just another guide filled with generic advice. It's a **unique blueprint for financial empowerment**, meticulously designed to equip you with the tools and strategies to take control of your finances and unlock your full potential.

You'll embark on a ten-step journey toward financial freedom in these pages. We'll delve into the importance of **transparency**, where meticulously tracking **every penny** in and out becomes the foundation for intelligent money management. You'll discover how to **categorize** your spending, revealing hidden patterns and areas for improvement. With this newfound awareness, we'll guide you through crafting a **realistic**

and achievable budget that prioritizes your needs while leaving room for savings and responsible enjoyment.

But budgeting without a plan is like building a house on sand. In this book, we'll explore powerful strategies like leveraging **fixed expense** management to your advantage and harnessing the power of **"no"** to curb impulsive spending. These strategies will **help you manage your money** better, reduce stress, and save valuable time.

This book isn't just about saving money and **building wealth**. We'll explore how to **reward yourself** for achieving financial milestones and keeping motivation high. Finally, we'll unveil the secrets of cultivating the **mindset of a wise spender, resourceful saver, and intelligent investor**.

Whether you're a college student just starting or a seasoned professional, "10 Strategies to Budget Your Money" offers valuable insights for every stage of your financial journey. **Let's embark on this journey together** and unlock the door to financial freedom, security, and the confidence to pursue your dreams.

ACKNOWLEDGMENT

Bringing this book to life was a journey made possible by the dedication and expertise of a phenomenal team. I offer my deepest gratitude to each of you.

Rhonda Brown, The Book Architect: Thank you for architecting many stories, including mine. Your guidance throughout the writing process, from brainstorming to polishing, was invaluable. Your passion for empowering others to write their stories is truly inspiring.

LaCheka Phillips, The Go 2 Chic of Everything AI: Your mastery of artificial intelligence was instrumental in ensuring my content was current and relevant. You helped me navigate the ever-evolving world of finance with cutting-edge knowledge.

Caliph Johnson, Health and Wellness Coach: Your dedication to well-being extends beyond the physical. You understand the connection between financial health and overall well-being, and your insights helped me craft a holistic approach to budgeting.

Miriam Smith, Executive Virtual Assistant: You are the magician behind the scenes. Your exceptional organizational skills and tireless assistance keep our project on track. Your ability to manage details always ensures a smooth and efficient process.

Anthony Jackson, Brand and Product Designer: Thank you for creating visually engaging merchandise that perfectly captures the essence of our projects. Your design expertise makes a powerful first impression and sets the tone for valuable financial strategies.

Thank you to my mom and sister for always believing in me. Your unwavering support and encouragement have been a constant source of strength, and I am forever grateful for your faith in my journey.

To my brother-in-law, thank you for being a good role model. Your integrity and dedication have set a high standard for me to follow, and I deeply appreciate your positive influence in my life.

Thank you for your unwavering support, expertise, and collaborative spirit to each of you. You are a necessary part of my journey, and I am incredibly grateful for your contributions.

INTRODUCTION

Welcome to "Mission to Millions: 10 Strategies to Budget Your Money." This book guides anyone looking to take control of their financial future and build wealth, regardless of their starting point. In a world with abundant financial challenges, understanding the principles of money management and wealth creation is more important than ever.

For years, I have worked with individuals and families, helping them navigate the complexities of personal finance. Through my journey, I have seen firsthand the transformative power of financial education. Whether burdened with debt, living paycheck to paycheck, or simply looking to improve your financial situation, this book provides the tools and strategies you need to succeed.

The title, "Mission to Millions," reflects the aspiration to reach financial milestones that may once have seemed impossible. It also acknowledges that wealth is about money and creating a fulfilling and secure life. These strategies are designed to help you build wealth sustainably and ethically, with a focus on long-term growth and stability.

This book is not a collection of theoretical concepts; it's a practical guide that offers actionable steps you can incorporate into your daily routine. Each chapter focuses on a specific aspect of personal finance, from challenging negative money beliefs to setting realistic financial goals, tracking expenses, and simplifying your lifestyle. We'll also explore various tools and platforms that can help you manage your finances more effectively and provide tips on saving money without compromising your quality of life.

Moreover, this book aims to empower you to make informed decisions and take control of your financial destiny. It encourages a mindset shift—seeing money as a tool for achieving your dreams rather than a source of stress or limitation. By the end of this journey, you will have a clearer understanding of your financial situation, a solid plan for your money, and the confidence to pursue your goals.

Financial success is not a privilege reserved for a select few; it is within reach for anyone who is willing to learn and take consistent action. I invite you to join me on this 'Mission to Millions,' where we will work together to build a brighter and more prosperous future. Let's embark on this journey to financial empowerment and uncover the true potential that lies within you.

Chapter 1

Transforming Your Financial Mindset

"Your financial future is determined by how well you manage the
pennies. Track them diligently, and you'll pave
the way for a prosperous tomorrow."
- Denzel Washington

Changing your thoughts about money is the first and most crucial step toward achieving financial success. Many people struggle with money due to ingrained negative beliefs, unrealistic goals, and a lack of awareness about spending habits. In this chapter, we will explore how to challenge negative beliefs about money, set realistic financial goals, utilize the best platforms to track expenses, discover easy ways to save money, simplify your lifestyle, and learn to say no gracefully when it comes to financial matters.

Challenge Negative Beliefs About Money

Negative beliefs about money often stem from childhood experiences, societal influences, or past financial failures. These beliefs can significantly hinder your ability to manage and grow your wealth. Common negative beliefs include:

- Money is the root of all evil.

- Rich people are greedy.

- I'll never be able to get out of debt.

- I'm not good with money.

To challenge these beliefs, start by identifying them. Reflect on your financial experiences and note any recurring negative thoughts. Once identified, reframe these thoughts with positive affirmations and evidence-based statements. For example, replace "I'm not good with money" with "I am capable of learning and improving my financial skills."

Engage in continuous learning about personal finance. Read books, take courses, and seek advice from financial experts. By educating yourself, you can build confidence in your ability to manage money effectively. Surround yourself with positive influences—people who have a healthy relationship with money and can offer support and guidance.

Set Realistic Financial Goals for Your Money

Setting realistic financial goals is essential for creating a roadmap to financial success. Your goals should be Specific, Measurable, Achievable, Relevant, and Time-bound (SMART). Here are some steps to help you set and achieve realistic financial goals:

1. **Identify Your Goals:** Determine what you want to achieve financially. This could include saving for a house, paying off debt, building an emergency fund, or investing for retirement.

2. **Break Down Goals:** Divide your larger goals into smaller, manageable tasks. For example, if your goal is to save $10,000 for a down payment on a house, break it down into monthly savings targets.

3. **Create a Budget:** Develop a budget that aligns with your financial goals. Track your income and expenses to ensure you save enough to reach your targets.

4. **Monitor Progress:** Regularly review your progress towards your goals. Adjust your budget and savings plan as needed to stay on track.

5. **Celebrate Milestones:** Acknowledge and celebrate when you achieve smaller milestones. This will keep you motivated and reinforce positive financial behaviors.

The Best Platforms to Track Expenses

Tracking your expenses is crucial for understanding where your money goes and identifying areas where you can cut back. Here are some of the best platforms to help you track your expenses:

1. **Mint:** Mint is a free budgeting app that connects to your bank accounts and credit cards, automatically

categorizing transactions. It provides a comprehensive overview of your spending habits and offers personalized tips for saving money.

2. **YNAB (You Need a Budget):** YNAB is a budgeting app that focuses on giving every dollar a job. It helps you allocate your income towards expenses, savings, and debt repayment, ensuring you stay within your budget.

3. **Pocket Guard:** Pocket Guard simplifies budgeting by showing you how much money you have available after accounting for bills, goals, and necessities. It also helps you identify areas where you can save.

4. **Personal Capital:** Personal Capital offers budgeting tools alongside investment tracking. It's ideal for those who want to manage their finances holistically, including retirement planning.

5. **Every Dollar:** Developed by Dave Ramsey, Every Dollar follows the zero-based budgeting method.

It's user-friendly and helps you plan for every dollar of your income.

Tracking your expenses is essential because it provides clarity on your spending patterns, helps you stay within your budget, and ensures you're making progress towards your financial goals. Regularly reviewing your expenses can also highlight unnecessary costs and areas where you can save.

Easy Ways to Save Money

Saving money doesn't have to be complicated. Here are some simple strategies to help you save more:

1. **Use Coupons:** Take advantage of coupons and discount codes when shopping. Apps like Honey and Rakuten can help you find deals and earn cashback on purchases.

2. **Cancel Unnecessary Subscriptions:** Review your subscriptions and cancel any that you don't use regularly. Streaming services, magazine

subscriptions, and gym memberships can add up quickly.

3. **Use a Grocery List:** Plan your meals and create a grocery list before shopping. This helps you avoid impulse purchases and stick to your budget.

4. **Avoid Fast Food:** Prepare meals at home instead of eating out. Cooking at home is usually healthier and more cost-effective.

5. **Skip Expensive Coffee Brands:** Brew your coffee at home instead of buying from expensive coffee shops. Invest in a good coffee maker and quality beans for a delicious cup of coffee.

6. **Take Your Lunch to Work:** Pack your lunch instead of eating out during work hours. This can save you a significant amount of money each week.

7. **Buy Generic Brands:** Opt for generic or store brands instead of name brands. They are often of similar quality but at a lower price.

8. **Shop During Sales:** Take advantage of sales events and clearance sections to purchase items at a discount.

Simplifying Your Lifestyle

Simplifying your lifestyle can lead to significant financial benefits. Here's how to streamline your life and save money:

1. **Declutter Your Home:** Sell or donate items you no longer need. This can create additional income and reduce the temptation to buy unnecessary things.

2. **Limit Social Media and Advertising Exposure:** Reduce your exposure to advertisements and social media that promote consumerism. This can help you avoid impulse purchases and focus on what truly matters.

3. **Prioritize Experiences Over Things:** Spend money on experiences, such as travel or hobbies,

rather than material possessions. Experiences often provide more lasting happiness and fulfillment.

4. **Adopt a Minimalist Mindset:** Embrace minimalism by focusing on owning fewer, high-quality items. This can reduce clutter and help you appreciate what you have.

5. **Reduce Energy Consumption:** Lower your utility bills by using energy-efficient appliances, turning off lights when not in use, and reducing water usage.

Learn to Say No Gracefully When It Comes to Money

Learning to say no gracefully is an important skill when managing your finances. Whether it's declining a social invitation that doesn't fit your budget or saying no to a loan request, here are some tips to help you:

1. **Be Honest:** Be truthful about your financial situation. You don't need to provide details, but a simple explanation can help others understand your decision.

2. **Offer Alternatives:** Suggest alternative activities that are more budget friendly. For example, propose a potluck dinner instead of dining out.

3. **Practice Politeness:** Use polite language and a friendly tone when saying no. This helps maintain positive relationships.

4. **Set Boundaries:** Establish clear financial boundaries and stick to them. Communicate these boundaries to friends and family so they know what to expect.

5. **Prioritize Your Goals:** Remind yourself of your financial goals and why it's important to stick to your budget. This can make it easier to decline requests that don't align with your priorities.

Conclusion

Transforming your financial mindset requires challenging negative beliefs, setting realistic goals, tracking your expenses, finding easy ways to save money, simplifying your lifestyle, and learning to say no gracefully. By implementing these strategies, you can take control of your finances and work towards a secure and prosperous future. Remember, financial success is a journey, and every small step you take brings you closer to your ultimate goals.

12

Chapter 2

Best Practices for Credit Cards

"Success is not an accident. It is hard work, perseverance,
learning, studying, sacrifice, and most of all,
love of what you are doing."

- Pele

What a Good Credit Profile Looks Like

Building a strong credit profile is essential for financial health and accessing various financial products at favorable terms. A good credit profile comprises several key components:

1. **100% Payment History:** The cornerstone of a robust credit profile is a perfect payment history. This means paying all your bills on time, every time. Lenders view a spotless payment history as an indicator of reliability and financial discipline.

2. **1 to 6% Credit Utilization:** Credit utilization refers to the percentage of your total available credit

that you are currently using. Maintaining a low credit utilization rate, ideally between 1 to 6%, shows that you are managing your credit responsibly without maxing out your cards.

3. **0 Derogatory Marks**: Derogatory marks include late payments, collections, bankruptcies, and other negative entries on your credit report. Avoiding these marks is crucial as they can significantly impact your credit score and take years to remove.

4. **6 Years Average Credit Age:** The age of your credit accounts contributes to your overall credit score. An average credit age of at least six years indicates a well-established credit history, which can be beneficial when applying for new credit.

5. **10 Open Accounts:** A mix of credit accounts, including credit cards, installment loans, and mortgages, demonstrates your ability to manage various types of credit. Having around ten open

accounts can show lenders that you have experience handling multiple credit lines.

6. **0 to 2 Inquiries:** Hard inquiries occur when a lender checks your credit report as part of the application process. Limiting the number of hard inquiries to two or fewer within a 24-month period can help maintain your credit score, as too many inquiries can suggest a high risk to lenders.

Using the Snowball vs Avalanche Method to Pay Debt

Paying off debt can be overwhelming, but two popular strategies can help you manage and eliminate your debt effectively: the Snowball Method and the Avalanche Method.

The Snowball Method

The Snowball Method focuses on paying off your smallest debts first, regardless of the interest rate. Here's how it works:

1. **List Your Debts**: Write down all your debts in order from smallest to largest.

2. **Make Minimum Payments:** Continue making the minimum payments on all your debts except the smallest one.

3. **Pay Extra on the Smallest Debt:** Allocate any extra money you have towards paying off the smallest debt.

4. **Move to the Next Debt:** Once the smallest debt is paid off, move on to the next smallest debt and apply the same strategy.

The Snowball Method is effective because it provides quick wins, giving you a psychological boost as you see debts disappearing. It's a great way to build momentum and stay motivated.

The Avalanche Method
The Avalanche Method, on the other hand, focuses on paying off debts with the highest interest rates first. Here's how it works:

1. **List Your Debts:** Write down all your debts in order from highest to lowest interest rate.

2. **Make Minimum Payments**: Continue making the minimum payments on all your debts except the one with the highest interest rate.

3. **Pay Extra on the Highest Interest Debt**: Allocate any extra money you have towards paying off the debt with the highest interest rate.

4. **Move to the Next Debt:** Once the highest interest debt is paid off, move on to the next highest interest debt and apply the same strategy.

The Avalanche Method is more cost-effective in the long run because you'll pay less in interest. This method is ideal for those who want to minimize the total interest paid and can stay committed without needing the quick wins provided by the Snowball Method.

Credit Card Stacking

Credit card stacking is a strategy used to obtain a significant amount of credit, typically ranging from $100,000 to $250,000, by applying for multiple credit cards in a short period. Here's how you can approach it:

1. **Assess Your Credit Profile:** Ensure your credit profile is strong, with a high credit score, low utilization, and no derogatory marks. This increases your chances of approval.

2. **Research Credit Cards:** Identify credit cards that offer high credit limits and favorable terms. Look for cards with low-interest rates, no annual fees, and generous introductory offers.

3. **Apply Strategically:** Apply for multiple credit cards within a short timeframe, usually within a day or two. This minimizes the impact of hard inquiries on your credit score.

4. **Maximize Approvals:** Start with cards that are more likely to approve you based on your credit profile. As you get approved, use your new credit limits to strengthen your profile for subsequent applications.

5. **Manage Your Accounts**: Once approved, manage your new accounts responsibly by maintaining low utilization, paying bills on time, and avoiding any actions that could negatively impact your credit score.

Credit card stacking can provide significant capital, but it requires careful planning and management to avoid potential pitfalls such as high-interest rates and overwhelming debt.

Utilize Cash Back and Reward Programs

Using credit cards with cash back and reward programs can be a smart way to earn money and benefits on your everyday purchases. Here are some top credit cards and their key benefits:

American Express Blue Cash Preferred® Card

- **6% Cash Back**: On U.S. supermarkets (up to $6,000 per year).

- **3% Cash Back**: On U.S. gas stations and transit.

- **1% Cash Back**: On other purchases.

- **Welcome Offer**: $300 statement credit after spending $3,000 in the first 6 months.

Chase Freedom Unlimited®

- **5% Cash Back**: On travel purchased through Chase Ultimate Rewards®.

- **3% Cash Back**: On dining and drugstore purchases.

- **1.5% Cash Back**: On all other purchases.

- **Sign-Up Bonus**: $200 bonus after spending $500 in the first 3 months.

Citi® Double Cash Card

- **2% Cash Back**: 1% when you buy and 1% when you pay off the purchase.

- **No Annual Fee**: A straightforward cash back card with no annual fee.

Capital One Venture Rewards Credit Card

- **2 Miles per Dollar**: On every purchase.

- **Bonus Miles**: 60,000 miles after spending $3,000 in the first 3 months.

- **Travel Benefits**: No foreign transaction fees and flexible redemption options.

Discover it® Cash Back

- **5% Cash Back**: On rotating quarterly categories up to $1,500 (activation required).

- **1% Cash Back**: On all other purchases.

- **Cash Back Match**: Dollar-for-dollar match of all cash back earned in the first year.

Wells Fargo Active Cash® Card

- **2% Cash Back**: On all purchases with no limits.

- **Welcome Offer**: $200 cash rewards bonus after spending $1,000 in the first 3 months.

- **0% APR Intro Offer**: 0% introductory APR for 15 months on purchases and qualifying balance transfers.

By strategically using these cards, you can maximize your cash back and rewards, turning your everyday spending into valuable benefits.

How to Use Interest-Free Credit Cards to Your Advantage

Interest-free credit cards offer an introductory period during which no interest is charged on purchases or balance transfers. Here's how you can use these cards to your advantage:

1. **Make Large Purchases:** Use an interest-free credit card to finance significant expenses like appliances, furniture, or home improvements. Pay off the balance within the introductory period to avoid interest charges.

2. **Consolidate Debt**: Transfer existing high-interest debt to an interest-free credit card. This can provide temporary relief from interest charges, allowing you to pay down the principal faster.

3. **Plan Ahead:** Before the introductory period ends, ensure you have a plan to pay off the remaining balance or transfer it to another card with a promotional offer.

Using interest-free credit cards wisely can save you money on interest and help you manage your finances more effectively.

Building Wealth Through Rental Properties

Investing in rental properties can be a lucrative way to build wealth, and using credit can help you get started. Here's how you can use credit to purchase multi-unit properties and start generating rental income:

1. **Assess Your Finances**: Ensure your credit profile is strong to qualify for favorable mortgage terms. A good credit score, low debt-to-income ratio, and substantial down payment can enhance your approval chances.

2. **Research Properties**: Look for multi-unit properties such as duplexes, triplexes, four-plexes, or apartment buildings. Consider factors like location, market demand, and potential rental income.

3. **Secure Financing**: Apply for a mortgage to finance your property purchase. Consider FHA loans, which allow for lower down payments, or conventional loans for higher credit profiles.

4. **Calculate ROI**: Analyze the potential return on investment (ROI) by estimating rental income, property expenses, and financing costs. Ensure the property will generate positive cash flow.

5. **Manage Your Property**: Once purchased, manage your rental property effectively. Screen tenants, maintain the property, and handle repairs promptly to ensure steady rental income.

6. **Consider Airbnb**: Short-term rentals through platforms like Airbnb can provide higher rental income, especially in high-demand areas. Ensure you comply with local regulations and provide a quality experience for guests.

Investing in rental properties can provide a steady stream of income and potential appreciation, helping you build long-term wealth.

By following these best practices for credit cards, you can maintain a strong credit profile, manage debt effectively, maximize rewards, take advantage of interest-free periods, and use credit to invest in rental properties. Each of these strategies can contribute to your overall financial health.

Chapter 3

Mastering the 72-Hour Rule
for Financial Success

"Every minute you spend feeling sorry for yourself
is another minute not getting better."

– David Goggins

In today's fast-paced world, the urge to make instant purchases can be overwhelming. Whether influenced by targeted advertisements, the latest trends, or a momentary desire, impulsive spending often leads to financial regret and instability. Enter the 72-Hour Rule, a powerful strategy designed to help individuals take control of their spending habits and make more deliberate, financially sound decisions. This chapter delves into the essence of the 72-Hour Rule, exploring its benefits and providing actionable insights on how to effectively implement it in your life.

Understanding the 72-Hour Rule

At its core, the 72-Hour Rule is a simple yet effective financial and decision-making strategy. It requires individuals to wait for 72 hours before making a purchase decision, particularly for non-essential or high-cost items. This deliberate pause serves as a buffer against impulsive buying behaviors, encouraging thoughtful reflection and more informed decision-making.

The First Step to Financial Freedom

Impulse control is a critical component of financial health. Impulsive buying can derail even the most carefully planned budgets and lead to financial stress. By implementing the 72-Hour Rule, individuals introduce a mandatory cooling-off period that helps curb impulsive buying tendencies. This period allows the initial excitement or desire for the item to subside, making it easier to evaluate the necessity and impact of the purchase rationally.

For instance, consider a scenario where you come across a flashy advertisement for the latest smartphone. The immediate urge might be to purchase it right away, driven by the fear of missing out or the allure of owning the latest technology. However, by applying the 72-Hour Rule, you give yourself the opportunity to step back, consider your current financial situation, and assess whether the purchase aligns with your long-term goals.

Reflective Decision-Making

One of the most significant advantages of the 72-Hour Rule is the time it provides for reflective decision-making. During the 72-hour waiting period, you can thoroughly evaluate the necessity and value of the potential purchase. This reflection period encourages you to ask important questions:

- Do I really need this item?

- How often will I use it?

- Does it align with my financial goals and priorities?

- Can I afford it without compromising my budget or savings?

By answering these questions, you ensure that your spending decisions are deliberate and aligned with your financial objectives. Reflective decision-making promotes a deeper understanding of your true needs versus wants, helping you avoid unnecessary expenditures that do not add significant value to your life.

Staying on Track

Budgets are essential tools for managing finances and achieving financial goals. However, spontaneous and unnecessary expenditures can quickly disrupt even the most well-planned budgets. The 72-Hour Rule acts as a safeguard, supporting better adherence to your budget by preventing impulsive purchases.

When you delay a purchase for 72 hours, you create an opportunity to review your budget and determine if the expense fits within your financial plan. This practice not only helps maintain budgetary discipline but also fosters a proactive approach to managing finances. By ensuring that every purchase is carefully considered and justified, you can avoid the pitfalls of overspending and stay on track with your financial goals.

Making Confident Choices

Buyer's remorse is a common experience that often follows impulsive spending. It is the regret or guilt felt after making a purchase that, upon reflection, seems unnecessary or unwise. The 72-Hour Rule significantly reduces the likelihood of experiencing buyer's remorse by promoting thoughtful and deliberate decision-making.

By waiting 72 hours, you allow time for the initial excitement or emotional impulse to fade. This cooling-off period provides a clearer perspective on whether the purchase is genuinely worthwhile. If, after 72 hours, you still feel confident about the decision, it is likely a well-considered choice. Conversely, if doubts arise during this period, it is a strong indication that the purchase may not be necessary or beneficial.

Financial Discipline Building Long-Term Habits

Financial discipline is crucial for achieving long-term financial stability and success. Consistently applying the 72-Hour Rule helps cultivate this discipline by encouraging mindfulness and intentionality in your spending habits. Over time, this practice becomes ingrained, transforming impulsive tendencies into deliberate financial behaviors.

Developing financial discipline through the 72-Hour Rule involves recognizing the importance of patience and self-control. It reinforces the idea that not every desire requires immediate gratification, and that thoughtful consideration leads to more prudent financial decisions. As this habit becomes second nature, you will find yourself making more strategic and goal-oriented financial choices, contributing to your overall financial well-being.

Redirecting Funds to Financial Goals

One of the most tangible benefits of the 72-Hour Rule is the potential for enhanced savings. By avoiding impulsive purchases, your free up funds that can be redirected towards more meaningful financial goals, such as building an emergency fund, investing, or paying off debts.

Consider the cumulative effect of avoiding small, impulsive purchases over time. A daily coffee shop visit, for instance, might seem insignificant on its own. However, by applying the 72-Hour Rule and opting to make coffee at home, you could save a substantial amount of money over a year. These savings can be redirected towards larger financial objectives, accelerating your progress towards financial security and independence.

Implementing the 72-Hour Rule

To successfully implement the 72-Hour Rule and reap its benefits, consider the following practical tips:

1. **Create a Waiting List:** Maintain a list of items you wish to purchase and note the date you first considered them. Review this list after 72 hours to determine if the desire for the item persists and if it aligns with your financial goals.

2. **Set Reminders:** Use reminders or calendar alerts to mark the end of the 72-hour waiting period. This ensures that you give yourself the full reflection period before making a decision.

3. **Evaluate Alternatives:** During the waiting period, explore alternative solutions that might fulfill the same need at a lower cost. This could include borrowing, renting, or finding a similar item on sale.

4. **Reflect on Past Purchases:** Periodically review your past purchases to identify patterns of impulsive spending and areas for improvement. Reflecting on previous decisions can provide valuable insights for future purchases.

5. **Involve a Trusted Advisor:** Discuss potential purchases with a trusted friend or family member who can offer an objective perspective. They may provide valuable insights and help you make more informed decisions.

6. **Focus on Financial Goals:** Keep your long-term financial goals in mind when considering purchases. Remind yourself of the importance of these goals and how impulsive spending can hinder your progress.

7. **Practice Gratitude:** Cultivate a sense of gratitude for what you already have. This mindset shift can reduce the urge to acquire more possessions and help you appreciate the value of intentional spending.

Conclusion

Embracing the 72-Hour Rule for Financial Success

The 72-Hour Rule is a powerful tool for managing impulsive spending and making more deliberate financial decisions. By introducing a mandatory waiting period before making purchases, you can significantly reduce impulsive buying behaviors, enhance budget adherence, and minimize buyer's remorse. This practice fosters financial discipline and mindfulness, ultimately leading to improved savings and financial stability.

As you incorporate the 72-Hour Rule into your financial routine, you will find yourself becoming more intentional and strategic in your spending habits. The benefits of this approach extend beyond individual purchases, contributing to a broader sense of financial empowerment and well-being. By mastering the 72-Hour Rule, you take a crucial step towards achieving your financial goals and building a secure, prosperous future.

Chapter 4

The Envelope System

"Most people can't retire after working 40 hours a week for 40 years and live on 40% of what they used to make. The 40/40/40 Plan: more myth than math!".

— Unknown

Managing personal finances can often feel overwhelming, but the Envelope System offers a simple yet powerful approach to budgeting. This method has stood the test of time due to its straightforwardness and effectiveness. The Envelope System involves categorizing your budget, using cash, maintaining spending control, providing visual accountability, encouraging savings, and allowing flexibility and adaptability. By adhering to these principles, you can achieve greater financial discipline and ultimately, financial freedom.

Budget Categorization

The core of the Envelope System lies in its categorization of expenses. At the beginning of each month, you divide your income into various spending categories, each represented by a physical envelope. Common categories include groceries, entertainment, utilities, and savings. This categorization is essential because it forces you to think critically about where your money is going. It also helps in ensuring that all necessary expenses are covered before any discretionary spending occurs.

For instance, you might allocate $500 to groceries, $200 to entertainment, $150 to utilities, and $100 to savings. These amounts are then placed into their respective envelopes. This approach not only organizes your finances but also creates a clear plan for your spending, making it easier to stick to your budget.

Cash-Based System

One of the distinguishing features of the Envelope System is its reliance on cash instead of credit or debit cards. At the beginning of the budgeting period, you withdraw the budgeted amount in cash and distribute it into the envelopes. This method is effective because it prevents you from overspending; once the cash in an envelope is gone, you cannot spend more in that category until the next budgeting period.

Using cash has a psychological effect that swiping a card does not. When you physically hand over cash, you feel the loss more acutely, making you more mindful of your spending. This heightened awareness can lead to more thoughtful and deliberate spending choices.

Spending Control

Spending control is a fundamental benefit of the Envelope System. By limiting yourself to the cash available in each envelope, you are forced to stay within your budget. This method effectively curbs impulse buying and overspending. If your entertainment envelope runs out of cash mid-month, you must either forgo additional entertainment expenses or reallocate funds from another envelope, making you more conscious of your financial decisions.

This enforced discipline helps you prioritize your spending. You become more aware of your financial limits and are less likely to make frivolous purchases. Over time, this control can lead to better financial habits and increased savings.

Visual Accountability

The physical envelopes provide a tangible and visual way to track your spending. Unlike using credit or debit cards, where transactions are often invisible and abstract, the Envelope System makes your spending habits visible. As you spend, you see the cash in the envelopes dwindle, which creates a stronger awareness of your spending.

This visual accountability can be a powerful motivator. When you see that your grocery envelope is nearly empty, it can prompt you to make more frugal choices at the store. Similarly, watching your savings envelope grow can be a rewarding experience, reinforcing positive financial behavior.

Encourages Saving

The Envelope System is not just about controlling spending; it also encourages saving. You can create envelopes designated for savings goals, such as an emergency fund, a vacation, or a major purchase. By allocating a portion of your income to these savings envelopes, you ensure that you are consistently setting aside money for future needs or financial objectives.

For example, if you want to save for a new car, you might allocate $50 each month to a savings envelope. Over time, this envelope will grow, bringing you closer to your goal. This method of incremental saving makes large financial goals more attainable and reduces the temptation to dip into your savings for non-essential expenses.

Flexibility and Adaptability

While the traditional Envelope System relies on physical cash and envelopes, modern technology offers digital adaptations that can provide the same benefits with added convenience. Numerous budgeting tools and apps mimic the envelope method, allowing for easier tracking and adjustment of budgets in real-time.

These digital tools can automatically categorize expenses, track spending, and provide alerts when you are nearing your budget limits. They offer the flexibility to adjust your budget categories as your financial situation changes, making it easier to stay on track. Whether you prefer the tactile experience of cash envelopes or the convenience of digital tools, the Envelope System can be adapted to suit your lifestyle.

Implementing the Envelope System Step-by-Step

1. **Assess Your Income and Expenses**: Start by calculating your monthly income and listing all your expenses. Be honest and thorough to ensure your budget is realistic.

2. **Create Budget Categories**: Divide your expenses into categories. Be sure to include both fixed

expenses (like rent and utilities) and variable expenses (like groceries and entertainment).

3. **Allocate Your Income**: Decide how much money to allocate to each category. Ensure that your total allocations do not exceed your income.

4. **Prepare Your Envelopes**: Label each envelope with a category name and the allocated amount. For digital systems, set up categories and budget amounts in your chosen app.

5. **Withdraw Cash**: For the traditional method, withdraw the total budgeted amount in cash at the beginning of the month and distribute it into the envelopes.

6. **Track Your Spending**: As you spend, take money from the appropriate envelope. For digital systems, log expenses in real-time to keep track of your spending.

7. **Review and Adjust**: At the end of the month, review your spending. Adjust your budget categories and amounts as necessary for the next month.

Real-Life Applications and Benefits

The Envelope System can be particularly beneficial for individuals who struggle with overspending or impulse buying. It provides a clear structure for managing money and reinforces financial discipline. Here are some real-life applications and benefits:

- **Young Adults and Students**: For those new to managing their own finances, the Envelope System offers a straightforward way to learn budgeting basics. It helps young adults and students develop good financial habits early on.

- **Families**: Managing household finances can be challenging, especially with varying expenses for groceries, utilities, and activities. The Envelope

System ensures that all necessary expenses are covered and helps families avoid debt.

- **Individuals with Irregular Income**: For freelancers, contractors, or anyone with an irregular income, the Envelope System can provide stability. By budgeting conservatively and saving in high-income months, they can ensure funds are available during leaner times.

- **Debt Reduction**: The Envelope System can be a powerful tool for those looking to pay down debt. By strictly controlling spending and allocating extra funds to debt repayment envelopes, individuals can make significant progress in reducing their debt.

Overcoming Challenges

While the Envelope System offers numerous benefits, it is not without challenges. Here are some common issues and strategies to overcome them:

- **Running Out of Cash**: If you run out of cash in an envelope, resist the temptation to borrow from another envelope. Instead, look for ways to cut costs or increase income.

- **Emergency Expenses**: Unexpected expenses can disrupt your budget. To mitigate this, create an emergency fund envelope and contribute to it regularly.

- **Consistency**: Maintaining consistency with the Envelope System requires discipline. Set reminders to track spending and review your budget regularly to stay on track.

- **Adapting to Digital**: Transitioning to a digital envelope system can be tricky for those used to cash. Start slowly by using digital tools for a few categories while keeping others as physical envelopes.

Conclusion

The Envelope System is a time-tested method that can transform the way you manage your finances. By categorizing your budget, using cash, controlling spending, maintaining visual accountability, encouraging savings, and embracing flexibility, you can achieve greater financial discipline and peace of mind. Whether you use physical envelopes or modern digital tools, the principles of the Envelope System can guide you towards a more secure and prosperous financial future.

Chapter 5

Zero Based Budgeting

"Success is to be measured not so much by the position
that one has reached in life as by the obstacles
which he has overcome while
trying to succeed."

— Booker T. Washington

Starting from Zero

Zero-Based Budgeting (ZBB) represents a fundamental
shift in how organizations approach their budgeting
processes. Unlike traditional budgeting, which typically
involves making incremental adjustments to the previous
year's budget, ZBB starts each new budgeting period from
a "zero base." This means that every expense must be
justified anew, without assuming that any past
expenditures are automatically valid for the future.

The concept of ZBB was first introduced in the 1970s by
Peter Pyhrr, an accounting manager at Texas Instruments.

He aimed to address the inefficiencies he observed in the company's budgeting process. By requiring managers to build their budgets from scratch, Pyhrr believed organizations could gain a clearer understanding of their financial needs and priorities.

In practice, ZBB involves a meticulous examination of all activities and expenses. Departments are not allowed to carry over last year's budget as a baseline. Instead, they must justify their budget requests in detail, explaining why each expense is necessary and how it contributes to the organization's goals. This rigorous approach encourages a culture of careful planning, prioritization, and resource allocation.

Justification of Expenses

At the heart of ZBB is the need for thorough justification of all expenses. Each department or unit within an organization must present a comprehensive explanation for every budget item they propose. This process begins with identifying and evaluating every activity that incurs a cost, from operational expenditures to capital investments.

The justification process can be broken down into several key steps:

1. **Activity Identification:** Departments must list all activities they plan to undertake in the upcoming period. Each activity is examined independently, without assuming any inherent necessity based on past practices.

2. **Cost Estimation:** For each activity, departments estimate the costs involved. This includes direct costs such as materials and labor, as well as indirect costs like overhead and administrative expenses.

3. **Benefit Analysis:** Departments must articulate the expected benefits of each activity. This involves demonstrating how the activity aligns with the organization's strategic goals and contributes to its overall mission.

4. **Prioritization:** Activities are then prioritized based on their importance and expected return on investment. This prioritization helps ensure that the most critical activities receive funding, while less essential ones may be reduced or eliminated.

This rigorous justification process encourages departments to critically assess their spending. It forces them to consider whether each activity is truly necessary and whether there are more cost-effective ways to achieve the same objectives. By scrutinizing every expense, organizations can eliminate wasteful spending and focus their resources on activities that drive the most value.

Resource Allocation

One of the primary benefits of ZBB is its ability to promote more efficient resource allocation. Traditional budgeting processes often perpetuate historical spending patterns, with incremental adjustments made each year. This can lead to the continuation of unnecessary or redundant expenditures, as departments may feel entitled to maintain their previous budget levels without rigorous scrutiny.

In contrast, ZBB requires a fresh evaluation of all expenses, fostering a more dynamic and responsive approach to resource allocation. By starting from zero, organizations can better align their spending with current priorities and needs. This can be particularly valuable in times of economic uncertainty or rapid change when past spending patterns may no longer be relevant.

Through the ZBB process, organizations can identify areas where resources are being underutilized or misallocated. For example, they might discover that certain projects are no longer delivering the expected returns or that some departments are consistently over-budget while others are underfunded. By reallocating resources based on current needs and priorities, organizations can optimize their use of funds and improve overall efficiency.

Additionally, ZBB encourages cross-departmental collaboration and coordination. Because all departments must justify their expenses, there is a greater emphasis on communicating and aligning their activities with the organization's broader strategic goals. This can lead to more cohesive and integrated planning, reducing duplication of efforts and enhancing overall organizational performance.

Alignment with Goals

A key advantage of ZBB is its ability to ensure that all spending is aligned with the organization's strategic goals and objectives. Traditional budgeting methods can sometimes result in a misalignment between spending and strategic priorities, as departments may continue funding activities that are no longer relevant or necessary.

In the ZBB process, every expense must be justified based on how it supports the organization's mission and objectives. This alignment is achieved through a detailed examination of each activity's purpose and expected outcomes. By requiring departments to demonstrate how their proposed expenditures contribute to the organization's strategic goals, ZBB fosters a more intentional and focused approach to budgeting.

This alignment process involves several critical steps:

1. **Strategic Planning:** The organization's leadership establishes clear strategic goals and priorities. These goals provide the framework for evaluating budget requests and ensure that all spending is directed toward achieving the organization's mission.

2. **Activity Alignment:** Departments must demonstrate how each proposed activity supports the organization's strategic goals. This involves mapping each activity to specific objectives and providing evidence of its expected impact.

3. **Performance Metrics:** To ensure accountability and measure progress, departments establish performance metrics for each activity. These metrics provide a basis for evaluating the effectiveness of spending and adjusting as needed.

By aligning spending with strategic goals, ZBB helps organizations focus their resources on the most critical areas. This can lead to better outcomes and a greater overall impact. It also encourages a culture of strategic thinking and planning, as departments are required to continually assess how their activities contribute to the organization's long-term success.

Focus on Efficiency

Efficiency is a central focus of ZBB. By examining all expenses in detail, organizations can uncover opportunities for cost savings and process improvements. This emphasis on efficiency helps organizations operate more effectively and maximize the value of their resources.

The ZBB process encourages departments to identify and eliminate inefficiencies in several ways:

1. **Cost Analysis:** By breaking down costs for each activity, departments can identify areas where

expenses are higher than necessary. This detailed cost analysis can reveal opportunities for reducing waste and optimizing spending.

2. **Process Improvement:** ZBB encourages departments to evaluate their processes and identify ways to improve efficiency. This might involve streamlining workflows, automating tasks, or adopting new technologies.

3. **Benchmarking:** Departments can compare their costs and performance metrics to industry benchmarks or best practices. This benchmarking process can highlight areas where the organization is lagging and provide insights into how to improve.

4. **Continuous Improvement:** ZBB fosters a culture of continuous improvement, as departments are required to justify their expenses and demonstrate efficiency every budgeting period. This ongoing evaluation and adjustment process helps

organizations stay agile and responsive to changing conditions.

By focusing on efficiency, ZBB helps organizations reduce costs and improve their overall performance. This can lead to significant savings and a more sustainable financial position. It also encourages a culture of innovation and continuous improvement, as departments are constantly seeking ways to enhance their processes and deliver better results.

Enhanced Accountability

Enhanced accountability is a significant benefit of ZBB. The requirement for detailed justifications and explanations for all budget requests fosters a culture of responsibility and transparency in financial management. This increased accountability helps ensure that resources are used effectively, and that spending aligns with the organization's goals.

In a ZBB framework, managers are accountable for the following:

1. **Detailed Explanations:** Managers must provide detailed explanations for their budget requests, including a clear rationale for each expense. This transparency helps ensure that all spending is carefully considered and justified.

2. **Performance Monitoring:** Managers are responsible for monitoring the performance of their activities and demonstrating how they contribute to the organization's strategic goals. This involves tracking performance metrics and reporting on progress.

3. **Budget Adherence:** Managers are accountable for adhering to their approved budgets and avoiding overspending. This requires careful planning and monitoring to ensure that expenses stay within the allocated limits.

4. **Continuous Evaluation:** Managers must continually evaluate their activities and expenses to identify opportunities for improvement. This ongoing evaluation process helps ensure that resources are used effectively and that any inefficiencies are addressed promptly.

By enhancing accountability, ZBB helps organizations maintain control over their finances and ensure that resources are used in the most effective way possible. This accountability also fosters a culture of responsibility and transparency, as managers are required to justify their spending and demonstrate their contribution to the organization's goals.

In summary, Zero-Based Budgeting offers a comprehensive approach to budgeting that can help organizations improve their financial management, resource allocation, and overall performance. By starting from zero, justifying all expenses, and aligning spending with strategic goals, ZBB encourages careful planning, efficiency, and accountability. This rigorous approach can lead to significant cost savings, better resource utilization, and a stronger alignment between spending and organizational priorities. Whether in times of economic uncertainty or growth, ZBB provides a valuable tool for organizations seeking to optimize their financial management and achieve their strategic objectives.

63

Chapter 6

Save 10% of Everything You Earn

"If there is no struggle, there is no progress."

— Frederick Douglass

Financial guru George S. Clason's timeless book, *The Richest Man in Babylon,* offers a wealth of wisdom on achieving financial security. One of the most fundamental concepts introduced is the principle of "paying yourself first," otherwise known as saving a consistent portion of your income. Clason emphasizes the importance of allocating at least 10% of your earnings towards savings, a practice he refers to as "fattening your purse."

Pay Yourself First

One of the most important financial principles you can adopt is to pay yourself first. This means prioritizing your savings as the first expense you handle with each paycheck. Imagine that you are the most important creditor in your life. When you earn money, the first ten percent should go straight into a savings account, even before you consider paying bills, buying groceries, or indulging in any luxuries.

Paying yourself first might seem challenging at first, especially if you're accustomed to spending freely. However, this practice sets the foundation for a solid financial future. The idea is simple: by treating your savings as a non-negotiable expense, you ensure that your financial health is prioritized above all else. Over time, this habit will become second nature, and you'll find that you can adapt to living on the remaining 90 percent of your income.

This concept was eloquently illustrated in "The Richest Man in Babylon," where the characters learned that their financial struggles were often due to failing to save consistently. By committing to save ten percent of their earnings, they began to see a significant improvement in their financial stability and overall wealth. This principle applies universally and remains relevant today.

To make this process easier, consider automating your savings. Set up an automatic transfer from your checking account to your savings account each time you get paid. This way, you won't even have to think about it, and your savings will grow consistently. Remember, the goal is to prioritize your future financial well-being, and paying yourself first is the most effective way to start.

Consistency

Consistency is the key to making the habit of saving ten percent of your income effective. It's not enough to save sporadically or when it's convenient. Financial security and wealth building come from disciplined and regular saving habits. No matter how much or how little you earn, setting aside ten percent consistently will accumulate over time and create a significant financial buffer.

To develop this habit, you need to treat your savings like any other recurring expense. Just as you wouldn't skip paying your rent or utility bills, you shouldn't skip paying yourself. It's crucial to save the ten percent before considering any other expenditure, regardless of your current financial situation. Even during tough times, maintaining this habit ensures that you're always working towards your financial goals.

Consistency also helps in building financial discipline. When you save regularly, you learn to live within your means. This practice not only helps in accumulating savings but also fosters a sense of financial control and responsibility. You'll find that over time, you're better able to manage your expenses and avoid unnecessary debt.

To stay consistent, track your progress. Keeping a record of your savings growth can be highly motivating. Whether you use a simple spreadsheet, a budgeting app, or a financial journal, seeing the incremental increases in your savings will reinforce your commitment to this habit. Celebrate your milestones and stay focused on the long-term benefits of consistent saving.

Financial Security

Saving ten percent of your earnings is not just about accumulating wealth; it's about achieving financial security. Financial security means having enough savings to cover emergencies, unexpected expenses, and future investments. It provides a safety net that protects you from the uncertainties of life.

Emergencies can happen at any time—a car repair, a medical bill, or a sudden job loss. Without savings, these situations can lead to financial stress and debt. By saving consistently, you create a buffer that allows you to handle these unexpected expenses without disrupting your financial stability. This security is invaluable, providing peace of mind and the freedom to navigate life's challenges more confidently.

Additionally, financial security opens up opportunities. When you have a solid financial foundation, you're better positioned to take calculated risks that can further improve your financial situation. Whether it's investing in a new business venture, pursuing further education, or making a significant purchase, having savings gives you the flexibility to make decisions that align with your long-term goals.

In "The Richest Man in Babylon," financial security is a recurring theme. The characters who diligently saved a portion of their income found themselves better prepared to seize opportunities and weather financial storms. This principle is timeless and remains a cornerstone of sound financial planning.

Mindset Shift

Adopting the practice of saving ten percent of your income requires a significant mindset shift. It's about moving from a mentality of living paycheck to paycheck to one of abundance and responsibility. This shift is crucial for long-term financial success and overall well-being.

When you prioritize saving, you start valuing your future self. This practice encourages you to think beyond immediate gratification and consider the long-term impact of your financial decisions. Instead of spending impulsively, you become more mindful of your expenses and more deliberate in your financial planning.

This mindset shift also fosters a sense of empowerment. Knowing that you're actively working towards financial independence can boost your confidence and reduce anxiety about money. You're no longer at the mercy of external circumstances; you're taking control of your financial destiny.

Moreover, this change in mindset can influence other areas of your life. The discipline and responsibility you develop through consistent saving can translate to better habits in health, relationships, and personal development. It's a holistic approach to improving your overall quality of life.

In "The Richest Man in Babylon," characters who adopted a savings mindset experienced profound transformations. They became more disciplined, resourceful, and forward-thinking. This mindset shift is a powerful catalyst for personal and financial growth, reinforcing the importance of saving as a fundamental practice.

Building Wealth

Saving ten percent of your income is the first step towards building wealth. When combined with wise investments, these savings can grow exponentially, leveraging the power of compound interest. Building wealth is not about making quick gains; it's about consistent, long-term growth.

Compound interest is a powerful tool for wealth accumulation. When you save and invest regularly, your money starts to earn interest, and over time, that interest earns interest. This snowball effect can lead to substantial growth, turning modest savings into significant wealth. The key is to start early and stay consistent.

Investing your savings wisely is crucial. Diversify your investments to spread risk and maximize returns. Whether it's stocks, bonds, real estate, or other investment vehicles, make informed decisions and seek professional advice if needed. The goal is to create a balanced portfolio that aligns with your financial goals and risk tolerance.

In "The Richest Man in Babylon," the characters who saved diligently and invested wisely were able to achieve significant wealth. They understood that wealth building is a gradual process, requiring patience, discipline, and informed decision-making. This principle remains true today.

Building wealth also means being proactive about your financial education. Stay informed about market trends, investment opportunities, and financial strategies. The more knowledgeable you are, the better equipped you'll be to make sound financial decisions that contribute to your wealth-building journey.

Investment Opportunities

By saving ten percent of your income, you position yourself to take advantage of investment opportunities that can further enhance your financial growth and stability. Having a financial cushion allows you to act when opportunities arise, whether it's investing in a new business, buying property, or capitalizing on market trends.

Investment opportunities often require capital, and without savings, you might miss out on potentially lucrative ventures. By maintaining a disciplined saving habit, you ensure that you have the necessary funds to seize these opportunities. This proactive approach can significantly accelerate your wealth-building process.

Moreover, being financially prepared allows you to invest from a position of strength. You can make decisions based on strategic planning rather than desperation or urgency. This mindset leads to better investment choices and reduces the risk of impulsive or poorly researched decisions.

In "The Richest Man in Babylon," the characters who saved diligently were able to invest in opportunities that others could not. Their foresight and discipline paid off, leading to substantial financial gains. This principle highlights the importance of being prepared and ready to act when opportunities present themselves.

To maximize the benefits of your savings, stay informed about potential investments and continuously educate yourself. Seek advice from financial experts, diversify your portfolio, and always consider the long-term implications of your investment decisions. By doing so, you'll be well-positioned to capitalize on opportunities and enhance your financial growth and stability.

In conclusion, saving ten percent of everything you earn is a powerful financial strategy that can lead to financial security, wealth building, and investment opportunities. By paying yourself first, staying consistent, fostering a mindset shift, and leveraging compound interest, you set the stage for a prosperous and secure financial future. The principles outlined in "The Richest Man in Babylon" remain timeless and relevant, offering valuable insights for anyone looking to achieve financial success.

Chapter 7

The 50/30/20 Rule Savings Plan

"Most people can't retire after working 40 hours a week for 40 years and live on 40% of what they used to make. The 40/40/40 Plan: more myth than math!".

— Unknown

Financial stability and growth are fundamental goals for many individuals and families. Achieving these goals can often seem complex and overwhelming, especially in a world filled with endless financial advice and strategies. However, one budgeting method stands out for its simplicity and effectiveness: the 50/30/20 rule. This chapter delves into the key aspects of the 50/30/20 rule, exploring how it can help you allocate your income wisely, reduce financial stress, and build a secure financial future.

The Foundation of the 50/30/20 Rule

The 50/30/20 rule provides a clear and straightforward method for managing your finances. It divides your after-tax income into three distinct categories:

1. **50% for Needs**

2. **30% for Wants**

3. **20% for Savings and Debt Repayment**

This structure allows you to prioritize essential expenses, enjoy non-essential items, and secure your financial future without the need for meticulous tracking of every penny.

Needs (50%): Essential Expenses

The first category, accounting for 50% of your after-tax income, is dedicated to your needs. These are the expenses necessary for basic living and meeting financial obligations. They include:

- **Housing:** Rent or mortgage payments, property taxes, and maintenance costs.

- **Utilities:** Electricity, water, gas, internet, and other essential services.

- **Groceries:** Food and household supplies that are required for daily living.

- **Transportation:** Costs associated with commuting, such as fuel, public transit, car payments, and maintenance.

- **Insurance:** Health, auto, home, and life insurance premiums.

- **Minimum Loan Payments:** Required payments on debts like student loans, credit cards, and personal loans.

Ensuring that these essential expenses are covered is the first step toward financial stability. By allocating half of your income to these necessities, you create a solid foundation for managing your finances.

Wants (30%): Enhancing Your Lifestyle

The second category, comprising 30% of your after-tax income, is reserved for your wants. These are non-essential expenses that enhance your lifestyle and bring enjoyment. Examples include:

- **Dining Out:** Meals at restaurants, cafes, and takeout.

- **Entertainment:** Movies, concerts, sports events, and streaming services.

- **Vacations:** Travel expenses, including flights, accommodations, and activities.

- **Hobbies:** Costs associated with personal interests and leisure activities.

- **Shopping:** Non-essential clothing, gadgets, and other discretionary purchases.

This category allows for flexibility and enjoyment without compromising your financial health. Allocating a portion of your income to wants ensures that you can indulge in life's pleasures while maintaining a balanced budget.

Savings and Debt Repayment (20%): Securing Your Future

The final category, making up 20% of your after-tax income, is focused on savings and debt repayment. This crucial portion of your budget is dedicated to:

- **Building an Emergency Fund:** Setting aside money for unexpected expenses, such as medical bills, car repairs, or job loss.

- **Contributing to Retirement Accounts:** Investing in 401(k)s, IRAs, or other retirement savings plans to secure your future.

- **Paying Down High-Interest Debts:** Prioritizing the repayment of debts with high interest rates to reduce financial stress and save on interest costs.

By consistently allocating 20% of your income to savings and debt repayment, you can build a strong financial foundation, reduce debt, and prepare for future financial goals and emergencies.

Adapting the 50/30/20 Rule

One of the greatest strengths of the 50/30/20 rule is its flexibility and simplicity. This budgeting method can be easily adapted to various income levels and financial situations, making it accessible to a wide range of individuals and families.

Adapting to Income Levels

Whether you are a high-income earner or living on a modest salary, the 50/30/20 rule can be tailored to fit your needs. The key is to adjust the dollar amounts within each category while maintaining the same percentage allocations. This ensures that your essential expenses are covered, your lifestyle is enjoyed, and your future is secured, regardless of your income level.

Adjusting for Financial Goals

The 50/30/20 rule also allows for adjustments based on specific financial goals. For instance, if you are aiming to pay off debt faster, you can temporarily allocate a higher percentage to the savings and debt repayment category. Conversely, if you have achieved a stable financial position and want to enjoy more of your income, you can increase the allocation for wants.

Simplifying Budgeting

The simplicity of the 50/30/20 rule lies in its straightforward approach. Instead of tracking every expense in detail, you only need to focus on three main categories. This makes budgeting less time-consuming and more manageable, allowing you to maintain consistent financial habits with minimal effort.

Long-term Financial Health: Building a Secure Future

Adopting the 50/30/20 rule is not just about managing day-to-day expenses; it's about promoting long-term financial health. By consistently allocating 20% of your income to savings and debt repayment, you can achieve financial stability and growth over time.

Building an Emergency Fund

An emergency fund is a crucial component of financial security. It provides a safety net for unexpected expenses, helping you avoid debt and financial stress during difficult times. Aim to save at least three to six months' worth of living expenses in your emergency fund. This will give you the confidence and peace of mind to handle any financial surprises that come your way.

Investing for Retirement

Planning for retirement is essential for ensuring a comfortable and secure future. By contributing regularly to retirement accounts, you can take advantage of compound interest and grow your savings over time. The earlier you start, the more time your investments have to grow, making it easier to achieve your retirement goals.

Reducing Debt

High-interest debt can be a significant burden on your finances. By prioritizing debt repayment within the 20% allocation, you can reduce the amount of interest you pay over time and free up more of your income for other financial goals. Focus on paying off high-interest debts first, such as credit card balances and payday loans, to maximize the impact of your repayments.

Setting Financial Goals

The 50/30/20 rule encourages you to set and achieve financial goals. Whether it's saving for a down payment on a house, funding a child's education, or starting a business, having a clear plan and dedicated savings can help you reach your objectives. Regularly review and adjust your goals to stay on track and ensure your financial plan aligns with your changing needs and priorities.

Promoting Financial Stability

Consistency is key to financial stability. By following the 50/30/20 rule, you develop disciplined spending and saving habits that contribute to long-term financial health. This approach helps you avoid living paycheck to paycheck and provides a structured framework for managing your money effectively.

Conclusion

The 50/30/20 rule is a powerful tool for achieving financial freedom. Its simplicity, flexibility, and focus on long-term financial health make it an ideal budgeting method for individuals and families alike. By dividing your after-tax income into three categories—50% for needs, 30% for wants, and 20% for savings and debt repayment—you can create a balanced and sustainable financial plan.

Embrace the 50/30/20 rule and take control of your finances. Prioritize essential expenses, enjoy life's pleasures responsibly, and secure your financial future with consistent savings and debt repayment. With this disciplined approach, you can build a strong financial foundation, achieve your financial goals, and enjoy peace of mind knowing you are on the path to financial freedom.

Chapter 8

The Jar System

*"I had to make my own living and my own opportunity.
But I made it! Don't sit down and wait
for the opportunities to come.
Get up and make them."*

— Madam C.J. Walker

The Jar System

In today's fast-paced world, managing personal finances can often feel like navigating a maze with no clear direction. Amidst this complexity, T. Harv Eker's "Jar System" offers a straightforward, yet profound approach to budgeting. This method, designed to help individuals take control of their financial destiny, divides income into six distinct categories, each represented by a jar. By following this system, you can ensure that all aspects of your financial life are adequately addressed, fostering a balanced and sustainable approach to money management.

Income Allocation: A Blueprint for Financial Health

The foundation of the Jar System lies in its methodical income allocation. By dividing your income into six specific categories, you gain clarity on how much money is available for different aspects of your life. This systematic approach not only helps meet your immediate financial needs but also encourages saving and investing for the future.

The six jars each serve a unique purpose: Necessities (55%), Financial Freedom (10%), Long-Term Savings for Spending (10%), Education (10%), Play (10%), and Giving (5%). This chapter will delve into each jar, exploring their significance and how to utilize them effectively.

The Six Jars: An Overview

1. Necessities Jar (55%)

2. Financial Freedom Jar (10%)

3. Long-Term Savings for Spending Jar (10%)

4. Education Jar (10%)

5. Play Jar (10%)

6. Giving Jar (5%)

Each jar plays a crucial role in your overall financial strategy, ensuring that every dollar you earn is purposefully allocated. Let's explore these jars in detail.

Necessities Jar

The Necessities Jar, comprising 55% of your income, is the bedrock of your financial plan. This jar is allocated to cover essential living expenses, such as rent or mortgage, utilities, groceries, transportation, and other necessary bills. By dedicating more than half of your income to these crucial expenses, you ensure that your basic needs are consistently met, providing stability and peace of mind.

To effectively manage this jar, track your monthly expenses meticulously. Use budgeting tools or apps to monitor spending and identify areas where you can cut costs. Remember, the goal is to live within your means while maintaining a comfortable lifestyle.

Financial Freedom Jar

Allocating 10% of your income to the Financial Freedom Jar is a strategic move towards achieving financial independence. This jar is dedicated to investments and wealth-building activities that generate passive income. By investing in stocks, bonds, real estate, or other income-generating assets, you create a financial cushion that grows over time.

The key to success with this jar is consistency and patience. Regularly contribute to it and reinvest the returns to benefit from compound interest. This disciplined approach can significantly enhance your financial security and pave the way to financial freedom.

Long-Term Savings for Spending Jar

The Long-Term Savings for Spending Jar also receives 10% of your income. This jar is earmarked for significant future expenses such as vacations, major purchases, or emergencies. By saving for these expenses in advance, you can avoid the stress of large, unexpected bills disrupting your monthly budget.

To maximize the effectiveness of this jar, set specific savings goals and timelines. For example, if you plan to buy a new car in three years, calculate the total cost and divide it by the number of months until the purchase. This will give you a clear savings target to aim for each month.

Education Jar

Personal growth and development are critical to long-term success, and the Education Jar, with its 10% allocation, supports this endeavor. This jar funds courses, books, workshops, and other educational expenses that enhance your skills and knowledge. Investing in yourself not only boosts your earning potential but also enriches your personal and professional life.

To make the most of this jar, identify areas where you want to grow and seek out relevant learning opportunities. Whether it's enrolling in a professional certification course or purchasing books on leadership, the goal is to continuously invest in your development.

Play Jar

The Play Jar, allocated 10% of your income, is designed for guilt-free spending on fun and leisure activities. This jar ensures that you enjoy life while managing your finances responsibly. Whether it's dining out, pursuing hobbies, or enjoying entertainment, this jar provides the funds for activities that bring joy and relaxation.

To use this jar effectively, plan your leisure activities within its budget. By doing so, you can indulge in your favorite pastimes without feeling guilty or financially strained. Remember, a balanced life includes both work and play.

Giving Jar

Finally, the Giving Jar receives 5% of your income. This jar is dedicated to charitable donations, gifts, or any other form of giving. Contributing to others fosters a sense of community and personal fulfillment, enhancing your overall well-being.

To maximize the impact of this jar, choose causes that resonate with you and support them consistently. Whether it's donating to a local charity, helping a friend in need, or participating in community service, the act of giving enriches both the giver and the receiver.

Implementing the Jar System

1. **Assess Your Income:** Begin by calculating your total monthly income. This includes your salary, freelance earnings, rental income, or any other sources of revenue.

2. **Allocate Your Income:** Divide your income according to the six jars. For instance, if your monthly income is $4,000, allocate $2,200 to Necessities, $400 to Financial Freedom, $400 to Long-Term Savings for Spending, $400 to Education, $400 to Play, and $200 to Giving.

3. **Set Up Separate Accounts:** To keep your finances organized, consider setting up separate bank accounts or using budgeting apps that allow you to categorize your funds. This helps you track your spending and ensure each jar is funded appropriately.

4. **Track Your Spending:** Regularly monitor your expenses and adjust your allocations if necessary. This ensures you stay within your budget and meet your financial goals.

5. **Review and Adjust:** Periodically review your financial situation and adjust your jar allocations as needed. Life circumstances and financial goals may

change, and your budget should reflect these changes.

Benefits of the Jar System

The Jar System offers several benefits, including:

1. **Clarity and Control:** By dividing your income into specific categories, you gain a clear understanding of where your money goes, allowing for better financial control.

2. **Balanced Spending:** The system ensures that all aspects of your financial life are addressed, promoting balanced spending and saving.

3. **Financial Security:** By consistently contributing to the Financial Freedom and Long-Term Savings jars, you build a financial cushion that enhances your security.

4. **Personal Growth:** The Education Jar encourages continuous self-improvement, boosting your skills and earning potential.

5. **Enjoyment and Fulfillment:** The Play and Giving jars ensure that you enjoy life and contribute to others, fostering personal satisfaction and well-being.

Overcoming Common Challenges

Implementing the Jar System may come with challenges, such as:

1. **Income Variability:** If your income fluctuates, adjust your jar allocations based on your average monthly income. This ensures consistency in your budgeting.

2. **Unexpected Expenses:** Life is unpredictable, and unexpected expenses may arise. Use the Long-Term Savings for Spending jar to cover these costs without disrupting your budget.

3. **Discipline and Consistency:** Maintaining discipline is crucial for the success of the Jar

System. Regularly review your budget and stay committed to your financial goals.

Conclusion

The Jar System by T. Harv Eker provides a structured, effective approach to managing your finances. By allocating your income into six distinct categories, you ensure that all financial needs are met while promoting balanced spending and saving. Embrace the Jar System and take control of your financial future, achieving both stability and growth in your financial life.

Chapter 9

Don't Rely on the 40/40/40 Retirement Plan

"Most people can't retire after working 40 hours a week for 40 years and live on 40% of what they used to make. The 40/40/40 Plan: more myth than math!".

— Unknown

What is the 40/40/40 Plan

Have you ever heard the dream of working 9 to 5 for 40 years, then magically retiring on a beach with a piña colada in one hand and your old paycheck in the other? Sounds pretty good, right? Well, that's the idea behind the 40/40/40 Plan. But here's the reality: it's more likely to leave you slinging burgers at 72 than sipping margaritas on a yacht.

Here's why the 40/40/40 Plan might not work for you:

- **Inflation Eats Your Money Alive:** Imagine this: you're making $50,000 a year now, and you dream of retiring on $20,000 (40% of your salary). But prices keep going up every year, like milk that mysteriously gets more expensive every time you go to the store. That means $20,000 in 20 years might not buy groceries, let alone a beach vacation.

- **Healthcare Costs Can Be a Monster:** As we get older, we tend to need more doctor visits and medications. Without your employer's health insurance plan in retirement, a big chunk of your retirement income might go towards keeping yourself healthy. That fancy beach house suddenly seems a lot less affordable.

- **Retirement Can Be More Expensive Than You Think:** Remember all those hobbies you dream of doing in retirement? Turns out, staying busy can cost money, too. Travel, activities, and even just the extra electricity from being home all day can add up quickly. The 40/40/40 Plan assumes you'll suddenly need less money in retirement, which isn't always true.

- **The Stock Market Isn't Always Sunny:** The 40/40/40 Plan assumes your investments will always grow steadily. But the stock market can be like the weather - unpredictable! A big crash right before you retire could seriously hurt your nest egg.

- **Work Can Give You More Than Just a Paycheck:** Think about it. Your job might give you a sense of purpose and social connection. Suddenly stopping work altogether could leave you feeling lost and unhappy.

So, what's the good news?

The 40/40/40 Plan can be a wake-up call! It highlights the importance of planning for retirement before it's too late. Here are some things you can do to get started:

- **Consider all the costs:** Think about inflation, healthcare, and the lifestyle you want in retirement.

- **Talk to a financial advisor:** They can help you create a plan based on your specific situation.

- **Start saving early:** The sooner you start, the more time your money has to grow.

Remember, retirement shouldn't be an emergency landing. With a little planning, it can be a smooth transition to a happy and financially secure next chapter in your life!

Building Wealth Through Rental Properties

Retirement. A time for relaxation, travel, and finally pursuing those passions you put on hold. But let's face it, a comfortable retirement requires a secure financial foundation. Rental properties offer a unique opportunity for retirees to generate steady income and build wealth for their golden years.

Here's how it works: you purchase a property, rent it out to tenants, and collect monthly payments. Ideally, the rent covers your mortgage payment, property taxes, and insurance, with some leftover cash flow. This positive cash flow is your reward for becoming a landlord.

Additionally, over time, the property value increase, allowing you to sell it later for a profit.

Why is this ideal for retirees?

Rental properties offer several advantages for retirees:

- **Supplemental Income:** Social Security and pensions may not cover all your retirement expenses. Rental income provides a reliable monthly income stream to supplement your existing retirement income.

- **Hedge Against Inflation:** Unlike some investments that lose value with inflation, property values tend to rise over time. This protects your investment and potentially increases your wealth.

- **Diversification:** Rental properties diversify your retirement portfolio, reducing your reliance on the stock market's volatility.

Getting Your First Rental Property

The first step is thorough research. Here's what you need to consider:

- **Market Analysis:** Research rental markets in your area. Look for areas with high occupancy rates, good schools (if targeting families), and growing job markets.

- **Financial Fitness:** Ensure you have a healthy credit score and enough savings for a down payment (typically 20% or more) and closing costs. Factor in ongoing expenses like property management, repairs, and vacancy periods.

- **The Right Property:** Look for well-maintained properties in desirable locations with good rental potential. Consider single-family homes, duplexes, or small apartment buildings depending on your budget and risk tolerance.

Remember, building wealth through rental properties requires a long-term commitment and ongoing management. However, with careful planning and execution, it can be a rewarding path to financial security in your retirement years.

How to Buy Partial Stocks on a Budget

Gone are the days when investing required a large amount to buy a whole share of expensive companies. Fractional shares have democratized the stock market, allowing you to invest with any amount you have available, regardless of a stock's price. This opens the door for budget-conscious investors to build a diversified portfolio and see significant returns.

Platforms like Robinhood, Stash, and M1 Finance have been at the forefront of fractional share investing. These user-friendly apps allow you to invest as little as $1 into companies like Amazon, Tesla, or Alphabet (Google's parent company), whose share prices might otherwise be out of reach. Imagine buying a fraction of Apple for $50 instead of needing the thousands required for a full share. This flexibility makes it easier to:

- **Diversify your portfolio:** By investing in slivers of various companies across different sectors, you spread your risk and are less vulnerable to the downturn of a single stock.

- **Invest consistently:** Fractional shares enable you to set up automatic deposits, say $25 every week, and gradually build your portfolio over time with a method known as dollar-cost averaging. This removes the pressure of timing the market perfectly and instills a disciplined savings habit.

- **Invest in high-growth companies:** Many of the most exciting and potentially lucrative companies carry high share prices. Fractional shares allow you to capture a piece of that growth potential without needing a large upfront investment.

Small Investments, Big Rewards

Let me share my experience. Since I started using fractional shares in 2020, my portfolio built on these platforms has grown by 17%. This handily beats the returns on my traditional 401K, which is tied to a more conservative mix of investments. While past performance is not necessarily indicative of future results, fractional shares have allowed me to participate in the growth of innovative companies I believe in, without breaking the bank.

By incorporating fractional shares into your investment strategy, you can unlock the potential of the stock market even with a limited budget. Remember, consistency and a long-term focus are essential for building wealth over time. So, take that first bite – even if it's just a slice – and watch your portfolio grow!

Keep the Change Investment Opportunities

Ever clean out your car and find a mountain of forgotten coins? Loose change seems like chump change – not worth the hassle of saving. But what if you could turn those pennies and dimes into a powerful tool for your future? That's where credit card "Keep the Change" programs come in.

These programs are like magic. They round up every purchase you make on your credit card to the nearest dollar. That spare change, your digital pennies, get automatically deposited into a savings or even an investment account. It's a painless way to save without even thinking about it!

Growing Your Acorn into an Oak Tree

Some Keep the Change programs just stick your money in a savings account. But others let you invest in it, which can be like planting a tiny acorn that grows into a mighty oak tree! Here's how it works:

- **Finding the Right Acorn Patch:** Look for banks or apps that partner with investment platforms. Popular options include Acorns (which works with many banks) or Bank of America's program which lets you invest your change in their Merrill Edge accounts.

- **Choosing Your Investment Adventure:** These platforms offer different "portfolios" like pre-made treasure chests, each with varying risk levels. Some are conservative, focusing on safety, while others are more adventurous, aiming for potentially bigger rewards (but also with a bigger chance of getting lost at sea). You choose the portfolio that matches your comfort level and financial goals.

- **Investing by the Penny:** A cool feature of Keep the Change investing is "fractional shares." Imagine buying a stock like a chocolate bar. Normally, you'd need the whole bar, but with fractional shares, you can buy a tiny piece (like a single Hershey's Kiss) with your spare change. This lets you invest even the smallest amounts, making every penny count!

The Good, the Bad, and the Penny Pinching

- **Effortless Saving:** Keep the Change investing is like setting your money on autopilot. No need to remember to transfer funds or worry about forgetting to contribute.

- **Long-Term Growth:** Remember the saying "time heals all wounds"? Well, it applies to money too! Even small amounts invested consistently can snowball into a big pile of cash over time, thanks to compound interest (like earning interest on your interest!).

- **Start Small, Dream Big:** Anyone can start building an investment portfolio with Keep the Change investing, no matter your income level. Every purchase adds up, making it an easy way to get into the investment game.

There's Always a Catch

- **Investing is Risky:** While potentially rewarding, investing always has some risk. The value of your investments can go up and down, and there's a chance you could lose money.

- **Credit Card Debt is the Enemy:** Don't forget, you're still using a credit card. To make this work, you absolutely MUST pay your balance in full each month.

- **Fees Can Nibble Away at Your Savings:** Some platforms might charge small fees for managing your account or investments. Make sure you understand the fees before enrolling.

Conclusion:

Credit card Keep the Change with investment options is a smart way to turn your everyday spending into a long-term financial benefit. By putting your spare change to work, you can watch your investments grow steadily, one round-up at a time.

Building Wealth with Cash Value Life Insurance

Life insurance might sound scary, like something you only think about when things get tough. But here's the secret: it can also be a tool to grow your wealth while protecting your loved ones. Think of it as a double win!

Regular life insurance is like a safety net, looking after your family if something happens to you. But cash value life insurance goes a step further. It's like a combination of that safety net and a growing piggy bank. Here's how it works:

- **Money Grows Over Time:** Unlike regular life insurance, cash value policies let your money grow over time. Imagine you pay a certain amount every month, like you would for any other insurance. But a portion of that money gets tucked away in a special account inside your policy. This account, like your own personal money pot, starts to grow with interest, building you a little nest egg.

- **Different Flavors for Different Folks:** There are a few different types of cash-value life insurance, each with its own style. Here's a quick rundown of the most popular ones:

  - **Whole Life:** This is the safe and steady option. Think of it like a high-yield savings account. Your premiums (monthly payments) stay the same, and your cash value grows at a guaranteed rate.

  - **Universal Life:** This one offers more flexibility. You can adjust your payments up or down depending on your situation. It's like having a savings account with a debit card – you can add more money when you have it and take some out if you need it (within limits, of course). The interest rate on your cash value isn't guaranteed, but it has the potential to grow faster than whole life.

- o **Variable Universal Life:** This is for the adventurous types. It lets you invest your cash value in the stock market, like buying shares in different companies. This has the chance of growing your money much faster, but also comes with the risk.

- **Turning Your Piggy Bank into a Cash Machine:** Here are a few ideas:

    - o **Borrowing from Yourself:** Most cash-value life insurance lets you borrow against your savings. The interest rates are usually lower than other loans, so it can be a good option for things like a down payment on a house or starting a small business. Remember, though, it's still your money you're borrowing, so pay it back to keep your policy healthy.

- Dividends - Some whole-life policies pay out dividends based on how the insurance company does. Think of it like a bonus! You can choose to have these dividends paid out to you for some extra cash flow.

- Stop Paying Sooner: By paying a little extra each month, you can grow your cash value faster. Once it reaches a certain amount, you might even be able to stop paying premiums altogether while your life insurance stays active. It's like paying off your car – eventually, you get to keep it without making monthly payments anymore!

The Big Takeaway: Patience is Key

Cash value life insurance is a great tool for building wealth, but it's a marathon, not a sprint. You need to be patient and plan for the long term. Talk to a financial advisor to see which type of policy is right for you, just like you'd talk to a mechanic before buying a new car.

Make Your Money Make Money for You

Life costs money. But what if your money could also be making you money, even while you're catching some ZZ's? That's the magic of passive income – income streams that require little to no effort to maintain.

Think of it like this: instead of your money sitting there like a lump of coal in your bank account, imagine it as a tiny worker bee, out there buzzing around and bringing you little bits of honey (cash) all the time. Passive income is like having a whole team of those busy bees working for you!

Passive income is like a superhero cape for your finances. It gives you a little extra cushion in case of unexpected bills or emergencies. Remember that leaky faucet you just had to fix? Passive income could help you cover that without throwing your budget into a tizzy.

Passive income can be the rocket fuel that propels you toward your financial goals. Imagine that dream vacation to Hawaii finally within reach, or maybe helping your kid with college costs. Passive income can help you get there faster.

Now, let's get down to business! Here are some side hustles you can try that won't take over your entire life:

- **Rent Out Your Stuff:** Do you have a spare room, a car that sits in the driveway most of the time, or even a parking spot you're not using? There are apps that connect you with people who are happy to pay you to use them! It's a great way to turn those unused things into cold, hard cash.

- **Become a landlord (of Sorts):** Have you ever considered renting a property? You can consider renting out a food cart to established vendors. They handle the food, you handle the cart, and everyone wins (especially your wallet with that sweet rental income).

- **Design and Sell Online (without the Hassle):** Feeling creative? Design t-shirts, mugs, or other cool stuff. Partner with a print-on-demand service and they'll make and ship your products. You design and collect your commission on every sale!

Remember, building passive income takes some effort upfront. It's not like planting a money tree and waiting for bills to sprout. But with a little planning and these handy side hustles, you can transform your money from a lazy lump of coal into a hardworking bee, buzzing away and building your financial future!

Chapter 10

Celebrate Your Success

"Discipline in budgeting is turning your thoughts and feelings into action to achieve financial results."

— - *Curtis G Martin*

Review the Progress You've Made on Your Financial Journey

Embarking on a financial journey is much like setting out on an adventure. It begins with a vision, an aspiration for a future that is financially secure and abundant. However, this journey is not a linear path. It involves numerous steps, obstacles, and milestones. To truly appreciate how far you've come, it's essential to take a moment to review the progress you've made.

When you first set out on this journey, you likely had specific goals in mind: paying off debt, building an emergency fund, saving for a significant purchase, or investing for the future. Reviewing your progress means taking stock of these initial goals and assessing how much closer you are to achieving them. Have you reduced your debt? Have you built a safety net of savings? Are your investments growing? Reflecting on these achievements, no matter how small, is vital.

Consider the habits you've developed and the financial education you've gained. Perhaps you've become more disciplined in budgeting, more knowledgeable about investments, or more conscious of your spending. Each of these represents a significant stride forward. By reviewing your progress, you acknowledge your efforts and build the confidence needed to continue moving forward.

Reinforce the Daily, Weekly, and Monthly Habits

Consistency is the cornerstone of any successful financial journey. It's the daily, weekly, and monthly habits that cumulatively lead to significant financial health. To maintain and reinforce these habits, it's essential to keep them at the forefront of your daily routine.

Daily Habits: Start by tracking your expenses every day. It may seem tedious at first, but this habit provides a clear picture of where your money is going. It helps you identify unnecessary expenditures and allows you to make informed decisions about your spending. Another daily habit is to review your financial goals each morning. This constant reminder keeps your objectives in focus and motivates you to make decisions that align with your goals.

Weekly Habits: At the end of each week, take time to review your budget. Compare your actual spending against your planned budget and make adjustments if necessary. This practice ensures that you remain on track and can address any discrepancies promptly. Another crucial weekly habit is to review your savings and investments. Ensure that your contributions are consistent and reflect any changes in your financial situation.

Monthly Habits: Monthly reviews are more comprehensive. This is the time to review all your financial accounts, including checking, savings, and investments. Assess your progress towards your long-term goals and adjust your plans as needed. Additionally, use this time to set new short-term goals for the upcoming month, ensuring they are aligned with your broader financial objectives.

By reinforcing these habits, you create a strong foundation that supports continuous progress. These consistent actions not only keep you on track but also help instill a sense of discipline and control over your financial life.

Reevaluate and Set New Short-term and Long-term Financial Goals

As you progress on your financial journey, it's essential to periodically reevaluate and set new goals. Your financial situation, priorities, and aspirations can change over time, and your goals should reflect these changes.

Short-term Goals: These are the goals you aim to achieve within the next year. They could include saving for a vacation, building an emergency fund, or paying off a specific debt. Evaluate your current short-term goals to see if they still align with your priorities. If you've achieved some of them, celebrate those successes and set new ones. If certain goals no longer seem relevant, don't hesitate to modify or replace them.

Long-term Goals: Long-term goals extend beyond a year and often include significant milestones such as buying a home, funding a child's education, or planning for retirement. These goals require careful planning and consistent effort. As your life circumstances change, it's crucial to revisit these goals and adjust them accordingly. Perhaps your retirement plans have shifted, or your priorities have changed regarding your child's education. Ensure that your long-term goals are flexible enough to adapt to these changes.

Setting new goals, both short-term and long-term, keeps you motivated and provides a clear direction for your financial journey. It's essential to make these goals SMART (Specific, Measurable, Achievable, Relevant, Time-bound) to ensure they are actionable and attainable.

Continuous Learning and Adaptation

The financial landscape is dynamic, constantly evolving with new opportunities and challenges. To navigate this landscape effectively, continuous learning and adaptation are crucial.

Stay informed about the latest financial trends, tools, and strategies. Read books, attend seminars, and follow reputable financial blogs and news sources. This ongoing education will empower you to make informed decisions and adapt to changes in the financial environment.

Consider learning about different investment options, tax-saving strategies, and innovative financial tools. The more knowledgeable you become, the better equipped you'll be to manage your finances effectively. Additionally, consider seeking advice from financial professionals. They can provide personalized guidance and help you navigate complex financial decisions.

Adaptation is equally important. As your financial situation and goals change, be prepared to adjust your plans. Flexibility allows you to respond to unexpected challenges and seize new opportunities. Embrace change as a natural part of your financial journey and use it as a chance to grow and improve.

Celebrate Your Success

Celebrating your success is a vital yet often overlooked aspect of the financial journey. Achieving financial milestones, no matter how small, deserves recognition and celebration. It reinforces positive behaviors and motivates you to continue striving towards your goals.

Start by acknowledging your achievements. Reflect on the progress you've made and the obstacles you've overcome. Celebrate the moments when you successfully stuck to your budget, paid off a debt, or reached a savings goal. These victories, big and small, are significant.

Find meaningful ways to celebrate. This could be as simple as treating yourself to a nice meal, taking a day off to relax, or planning a small getaway. The key is to choose celebrations that don't undermine your financial goals. Celebrating responsibly ensures that you stay on track while still enjoying the fruits of your labor.

Sharing your successes with others can also be incredibly rewarding. Share your achievements with friends and family who have supported you along the way. Their encouragement and recognition can boost your morale and strengthen your resolve to continue your financial journey.

Giving Back

An essential aspect of financial success is the ability to give back to your community. As you achieve financial stability and abundance, consider how you can make a positive impact on the lives of others.

Giving back can take many forms. It could be donating to a charity that you're passionate about, volunteering your time and skills, or supporting local initiatives. The act of giving not only helps those in need but also fosters a sense of purpose and fulfillment in your life.

Consider setting aside a portion of your income specifically for charitable giving. This practice ensures that giving back becomes a regular part of your financial plan. Additionally, involve your family in these efforts. Teaching your children the importance of generosity and community involvement instills valuable values that they will carry forward.

Beyond financial contributions, think about how you can share your knowledge and experience. Mentoring others, offering financial literacy workshops, or simply sharing your financial journey can inspire and empower those around you.

Conclusion

The journey to financial success is multifaceted, involving careful planning, consistent habits, continuous learning, and the ability to adapt to change. As you progress on this journey, it's crucial to periodically review your achievements, reinforce positive habits, set new goals, and remain committed to continuous improvement. Celebrating your successes along the way not only provides motivation but also acknowledges the hard work and dedication required to achieve financial stability.

Finally, remember that true financial success is not just about accumulating wealth for yourself. It's about using your resources and knowledge to make a positive impact on the lives of others. By giving back to your community, you create a ripple effect of positive change, fostering a sense of purpose and fulfillment that transcends financial success.

Embrace this journey with determination and optimism, knowing that each step brings you closer to the financial freedom and security you aspire to achieve. Celebrate your progress, stay committed to your goals, and use your success to uplift others. Your financial journey is a testament to your resilience and dedication, and it has the power to inspire and transform not just your life, but the lives of those around you.

About The Author

Curtis G. Martin is a dynamic entrepreneur, trainer, speaker, and business owner with over 20 years of experience as an instructor in Financial Literacy, Credit Repair, and Refinery Safety. An award-winning author, Curtis has penned five books and collaborated on two additional works, establishing himself as a thought leader and influencer in his field.

Originating from South Central Los Angeles, Curtis has devoted his life to self-improvement and community service. His role as a beacon of motivation and mentorship has spanned over two decades, guiding individuals toward personal development and growth.

As the Co-founder of The B.L.A.C.K. Masterminds Non-Profit Organization and the proud owner of a Craft and Safety Training Company, Curtis focuses on creating business opportunities and fostering a spirit of entrepreneurship. His innovative training programs empower families to utilize highly impactful breakthrough processes to rewire their brains, enabling them to experience immediate and long-term transformations. These changes include achieving higher incomes, increased net worth, more fulfilling relationships, personal power, and a profound sense of inner peace.

Curtis's collaboration with a leading personal and business development company has significantly expanded his reach, impacting millions of lives globally. His unique training style, which combines enjoyment with invaluable information, is his hallmark.

His expertise has been sought after by major corporations such as Exxon Mobil, Chevron, Valero, OSCA, Aera Energy, and BLACKS in Government. Curtis has also contributed to his community through initiatives like Marathon's Youth Program, which provides summer jobs for youth and young adults, demonstrating his commitment to giving back.

Curtis G. Martin's journey is a testament to the power of perseverance, education, and the unwavering belief in individuals' potential to achieve greatness. His work continues to inspire and transform lives, making a lasting impact on everyone he touches.

Made in the USA
Columbia, SC
20 August 2024

40302185R00085